Bush

The Australian bush is home to many plants and animals that can only be found in that environment. One of my favourite things to do is to walk in the bush and look out for this unique flora and fauna. I especially love to go night-spotting in the bush. This book is set at night, which is when nocturnal fauna are busy finding food ... and sometimes even making bush music!

Do you like bushwalking too? Next time you take a hike, keep your eyes open for plants, rocks and creatures. Some of them may be hard to find. Some cannot be found anywhere else in the world. You could keep a diary of what you see and hear every time you visit, particularly when you go at different times of the day. You might be surprised by how many new things you discover!

We all need to do what we can to protect the future of our unique bush and the animals that live there. Some of the animals in this book are endangered, such as the bilby, bandicoot and numbat. We have to look after their world and take care of them as best we can.

Jess Racklyeft

First published in Australia in 2023 by Affirm Press,
a Simon & Schuster (Australia) Pty Limited company
This edition published in 2025.
Bunurong/Boon Wurrung Country
28 Thistlethwaite Street, South Melbourne VIC 3205
Affirm Press is located on the unceded land of the Bunurong/Boon Wurrung peoples of the Kulin Nation.
Affirm Press pays respect to their Elders past and present.
AFFIRM PRESS and design are trademarks of Affirm Press Pty Ltd, Inc., used under licence by Simon & Schuster, LLC.
10 9 8 7 6 5 4 3 2 1

9781761820113 (paperback)
Cover design by Hannah Janzen
Printed and bound in China by RR Donnelley Asia

At times in this big universe
you can feel rather small.

But there are worlds of every size to see,
worlds for each and all.

Look up to watch the meteors
and satellites zip by.
Planets spin around their suns while
constellations light the sky.

That great big sky of stars is full
of planets still unknown.
But in the dark is one we know,
the place we call our home.

Soon it's time for us to snooze –
goodnight, setting sun!
The dusky sky wakes kangaroos,
hopping one-by-one.

A world of wild bushland stirs
beneath a rising moon.
Koalas stretch and wombats dig,
and dingoes start to croon.

Out on the highest branches find
a busy, hungry bunch ...
possums, gliders, flying bats
all munch their midnight lunch.

Bandicoot, snake, wolf spider
and screaming bush curlew,
sliding, searching, snuffling ...
a busy night-time crew!

There's a world underwater where
platypus make a splash.
Shrimp zip away just in time,
frogs make a slippery dash.

Find a smaller world beside
that muddy bushland creek.
Spot shiny golden beetles and
hear chirps and tiny squeaks.

Keep on listening for the little.
From red earth, cicadas sing!
A grasshopper symphony
sounds from legs and wings.

A brand new day is dawning now –
good morning, rising sun!
This wild world of bushland is ...

To Lucas from Aunty Jess
a home for everyone.